What's UP?

MICK MANNING AND BRITA GRANSTRÖM

W

F Schools Library and Information Services TS

What's up?
Let me climb on your
shoulders and see...

Some people grow taller than others!

Stairs!

Hurry up the stairs, two at a time to the top!

What could be higher?

Escalators are moving stairs that carry us from one floor to another.

4

Trees, growing tall and strong!
Let's climb the tallest, strongest tree...
What could be higher?

Trees are the tallest living things on Earth.

6

An old tower on a hill!
Let's dash up there and peer out
from the top...
What could be higher?

Until only about a hundred years
ago the tallest buildings were ....castles ...... cathedrals...

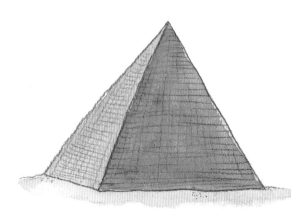

... temples...and the pyramids!

A shining skyscraper!
Let's ride in a lift, push a button to the top floor...
What could be higher?

Skyscrapers are the tallest modern buildings. They are made of strong steel and concrete.

A rocky mountain!
I'll race you to the topmost
snowy peak...
What could be higher?

Mountains are the tallest things on Earth.
The highest mountain is Mount Everest in Asia.

Clouds, hurrying by!
We can rise high in a balloon,
up through the fluffy clouds...
What could be higher?

Clouds are made from tiny drops of water — they float high above the ground.

Planes!
Let's whizz in our plane through the sky...
What could be higher?

Humans have tried to fly like birds for hundreds of years!

This is one of the first aircraft!

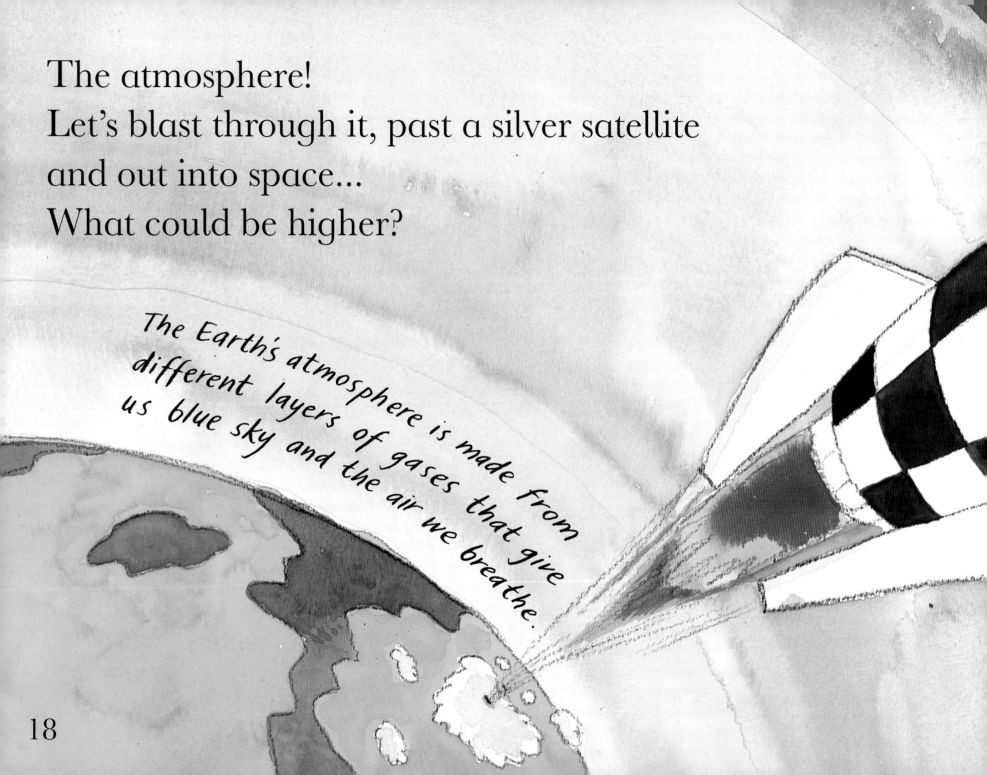

The atmosphere!
Let's blast through it, past a silver satellite
and out into space...
What could be higher?

The Earth's atmosphere is made from different layers of gases that give us blue sky and the air we breathe.

18

Satellites bounce messages around the world.

19

The moon!
Let's walk on the moon's surface ...
What could be higher?

Humans have explored the moon.
They found it was a desert land
of rocks with no air and no life

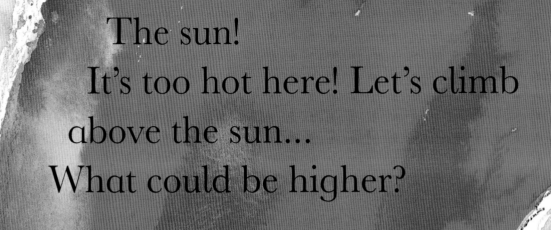

The sun!
It's too hot here! Let's climb
above the sun...
What could be higher?

The sun is a giant ball of fiery gas that heats our planet and gives us light.

Stars!
Millions of stars twinkling in deep space...
What could be higher?

Stars only seem small because they are so far away—
they are actually huge suns, some much bigger than our sun!

Even the nearest stars are so far away in space that even if you flew in a space rocket you would die of old age before you reached them!

Nobody knows of anything higher or further away than stars.
It's so empty and dark and lonely up here...

Let's race home!
Past the sun, moon, satellite, atmosphere, clouds, mountain, skyscraper, old tower, tree, stairs... until we are back with our feet on the ground!

what's UP?

deep space

sun

stars

moon

satellite

rocket

atmosphere

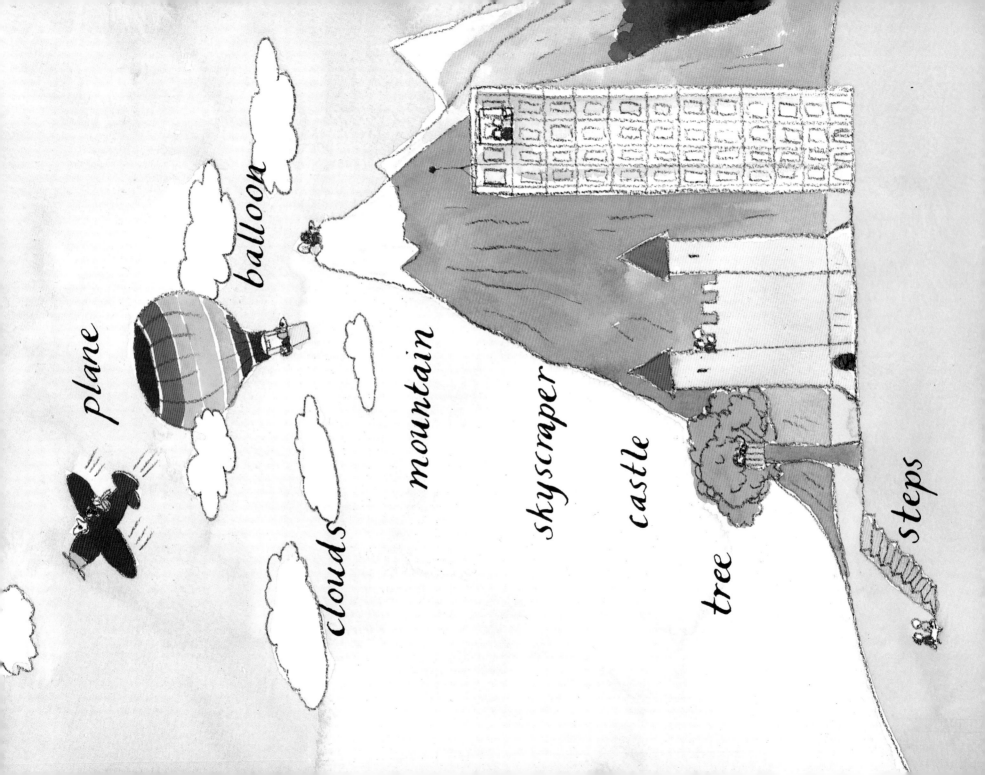

plane

balloon

clouds

mountain

skyscraper

castle

tree

steps

Helpful words

Atmosphere is all the sky above our heads and all the air that surrounds the Earth (page 18).

Gas is usually invisible, but it is everywhere! The air around us is made up of three main gases (page 18).

Hot air balloons are filled with air heated by flames from a gas burner. The hot air makes them float. Balloons can float very high and travel long distances very gently (page 14).

Moon is a huge lump of rock that circles our Earth (page 20).

Pyramids were built thousands of years ago by the Ancient Egyptians. They were built as tombs for kings (page 9).

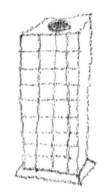

Satellites are machines in space that can bounce messages from computers or TV stations from one place on Earth to another. They can also send back pictures of the weather on Earth (page 19).

Skyscrapers are made of steel and concrete. They sway gently in the wind but they don't topple over (page 10).

Space is everything that is beyond our atmosphere. Space has no air to breathe (page 19-25).

Stars are other suns so far away they look like tiny dots of light (page 24).

Sun is a giant ball of fiery gas that gives us light and heat energy (page 22).

Towers usually belong to buildings like castles, churches or temples (page 9).

For Calle

This edition 2014

First published by Franklin Watts,
338 Euston Road, London NW1 3BH

Franklin Watts Australia,
Level 17 / 207 Kent Street, Sydney NSW 2000

Text and illustrations © 1997 Mick Manning and Brita Granström
Notes and activities © 2004, 2014 Franklin Watts

The illustrations in this book were made by Brita and Mick.
Find out more about Mick and Brita at www.mickandbrita.com

Series editor: Paula Borton
Art Director: Robert Walster
Consultant: Peter Riley

A CIP catalogue record is available from the British Library.
Dewey Classification 500

Printed in China

ISBN 978 1 4451 2886 3

Franklin Watts is a division of Hachette Children's Books,
an Hachette UK company. www.hachette.co.uk